Leads For Days

The Complete Guide to Creating
**Kick Ass Social Media Marketing
Campaign**

CHRISTINA FRISCIA

ISBN: 9781691890705

DEDICATION

Dedicated to every hungry entrepreneur on their grind.

It's all worth reaching for.

CONTENTS

ACKNOWLEDGMENTS

I acknowledge with great joy and pleasure:

- The friends who offered up help throughout the years when I didn't have two pennies to rub together. You were my motivation to uplevel.

- The family who ignored my texts and calls during hard times. You were my motivation to uplevel.

- The lovers who stepped on my goals and dreams because they wanted to see me do well, but never better than them. You were my motivation to uplevel.

- The inspired readers who have their hands on this book, who want a brighter future than they presently see. You are my motivation to keep going.

FOREWORD

It's 2013. I'm 24 years old. No job prospects really. Dead broke, no more credit to use, and I get the brilliant idea to get my real estate license. It was better than nothing, and seemed like a good backup to have in case I needed it.

I make the drive from Staten Island to Brooklyn several times a week for several months to take classes. Eventually, I take my school and state exams. Pass both, and quickly get hired at a boutique real estate brokerage on Wall Street in Manhattan.

For such an uppity brokerage, they certainly had no idea what was going on in the world of social media, but who was I to suggest anything new? I'm barely there 2 weeks, and I've gone through all their training requirements, spent hundreds of dollars joining REBNY and signing up for every apartment listing website they required of us.

My manager at the time was an older man named Michael. I adored him, because he was so traditional and old fashioned. Keep in mind, at this time, half of my head was shaved, and I had a full sleeve of fresh tattoos that were not about to be hidden in 98 degree NYC heat in the middle of July.

He knew very quickly that I was not down with the

methods this brokerage was teaching us as mandatory to advertise our new real estate businesses. I was broke. I didn't have hundreds of dollars a month to spend marketing these open listings in Manhattan.

"Use your network. Email at least 10 people a day."
Ok, I have like 10 friends altogether. So that gives me a day's worth of networking…

"Ask for referrals."
Easier said than done when I haven't done anything worth referring yet.

"Post 50+ listings per day on all the sites, and buy Craigslist credits from us for $10/posting."
You mean, advertise the same "deals" that 25,000 other NYC agents are advertising? Yet no one wonders why everyone thinks Craisgslist is scam city.

None of this made sense to me. It seemed like they wanted us to become our own business and brand, but we were advertising everything BUT ourselves!

How do I show these people how awesome I am, and how do I convey this energy through NakedApartments.com and Craigslist? Well, I can't.

But what I can do is use the one thing I know like the back of my hand- social media.

I wound up leaving this brokerage after about 2 months. Nothing was in alignment, and quite frankly, I couldn't afford to advertise anymore when all the leads that called just wanted a no fee, super inexpensive apartment. Rental clients have absolutely no loyalty. I learned this the hard way after spending the last $5 I had to my name to run uptown on the subway, only to have the client no call-no show, and later text me saying they found an apartment on their own and didn't need my services anymore.

A punch in the throat would've felt better than I did in that moment. Dripping sweat, running out of the 92nd Street Subway Station to make sure I'm outside the apartment to meet the client, and they totally flake on me.

I had no way to even get home. Not $1 in my pocket. Fantasizing about a stray $20 bill blowing down the street. What was I going to do? I failed myself. But I still had hope. Hope that something greater would come and I knew I just had to keep the faith alive that it would, and believe with my whole heart that it was all possible for me.

I pleaded with the express bus driver to let me on, saying I lost my wallet and needed to get home. The perks of being a 24 year old girl- he let me on. But I knew at that point I had to make a serious change.

I took a day or two to feel bad for myself, and decided to dedicate this newly found free time I had acquired to learning everything I needed to know about social media, digital marketing, and branding myself and my business online.

What I found blew me away. Learning what a sales funnel was, was like a light had switched on in my head. THIS IS WHAT MY BUSINESS WAS MISSING!

Setting up a sales funnel gave me the opportunity to establish myself as the go-to person in my area, and gave me the ability to brand myself how I saw fit, and represent myself the way I wanted to online. It was about providing value before asking for the deal. It was about playing the long game and consistently showing up, all while automating the lead generation part of the business.

This meant I could spend less time looking for clients, and more time servicing them. What a relief!

You mean, I could spend the price of a Starbucks drink everyday on Facebook Ads, and be seen by more people than the other traditional listing sites could ever generate?!

Sign me up!

It took some time, some testing, some failing and some succeeding, but once I struck gold with my ad campaigns, I was ready to show the world what was possible.

I randomly got hired to work at a real estate based creative marketing agency, and was put in charge of creating an ad campaign for a brand new luxury apartment complex in King of Prussia, PA.

You mean, I can test my concepts and strategies, while spending someone else's ad dollars?! YES!

By implementing my ideas and being determined to show how incredible this all was, I was able to bring in this development hundreds of leads over the course of one month, and wound up creating the campaign that would later totally lease out their space, before the last building was even finished.

This gave me the momentum I needed to bring in more clients, and the rest is history!

By being a rebellious and broke young girl, it gave me the opportunity to fall into what I do now, and LOVE to do: create killer social media marketing campaigns for businesses who need leads but have no idea how to utilize social media to do this.

In this book, you will find absolutely everything you need to start running your own profitable and highly converting social media marketing and sales funnel campaign, and start bringing in leads on autopilot.

What would just 20 more leads/month do for your business?

I'll show you the method to my madness next.

1. Intro To Facebook Marketing

Intro To Business Pages

To start off, when building an effective Facebook Marketing strategy, it's important to distinguish the difference between your personal Facebook page and your Business page.

You technically shouldn't be posting business related items to your personal profile. It's not likely that Facebook HQ would take down your personal profile due to violating their service agreement, but they would have every right to do so if they really wanted to. Facebook has also been cracking down on running ads without setting up your business page through the Facebook Business Manager, so it's important that when we start, we set it all up correctly.

Therefore, let's get that Business Page set up ASAP! Head over to Facebook Business Page to create your page. Once you have that done, you'll want to set it up with the Facebook Business manager. To do this, you'll want to go to Business.Facebook.com. This is going to be your main point of access for creating your ads, managing your billing and business settings, and basically anything that involves running your business page itself. It's important you set your page an ad account up with the Business Manager before doing anything   else.

After this is all set up, you'll want to start funneling your traffic directly to your business page. The big difference between your personal profile and your business page, and the main reason most agents just end up using their personal profile is because in order for your business page posts to be seen, it's kind of a "pay to play" type of thing. Meaning, Facebook prioritizes the accounts that put money into

Facebook before the accounts that just do free posting. (The way of the world these days.)

Yes, it will help to have people following your business page, but long term, that's not going to be enough to cut it. You'll need to implement some effective Facebook Ads to get your business page posts seen.

What Facebook has started fairly recently, is monitoring exactly what shows up in your news feed. Personal and posts from friends & family appear up top, followed by Facebook Ads and paid content, with organic business page posts trickling through at the bottom. More often than not, Facebook doesn't really even show those types of posts to your main audience. This is why many agents find it easier to just post from their personal accounts, but with that said, you can only be seen by the amount of people who are on your friends list (no more than 5,000) and that leaves a lot to be desired when running an ad can get you in front of THOUSANDS of different people instead. It's a necessary evil, and something that sometimes takes some mental adjusting, but it's well worth it to make the shift.

Would you rather market to the same people all day, who most likely are not even in the market for your service at this time, or would you rather get your ads seen by thousands of people who are in the market to move right now, have been searching online for a new home on various websites, and live in the area in which you focus? I think it's a no-brainer.

The Perfect Business Page

An informative and on brand business page is the foundation of a great Facebook and social media marketing strategy. It's what everything falls back on, and must leave a good and lasting impression on everyone who sees it. So, how do we do this?

Uplevel Your Cover Photo

Canva is your one-stop-shop for all things design and marketing, especially Facebook marketing. Creating your own engaging cover photo is super easy. They have the hard work done for you. No more guessing dimensions. Templates are created for you to plug and play. Simply type Facebook in the search bar, and you'll find templates for a cover photo and anything else you'll ever need to ramp up your marketing efforts.

Your cover photo should be unique, engaging, on brand, and include some kind of call to action or tagline describing your services. Once you've designed your cover photo using one of Canva's easy to customize templates, make sure it's easily readable from a mobile device. You can share the photo to yourself by clicking the "Share" button on top of the page, and emailing it to yourself, or others if you want outside opinions. Try uploading it to your Facebook business page, and make sure everything is easy to read and visually appealing from a mobile device, as this is typically where people are going to view your page from.

Polish Up Your Cover Photo

Your profile picture for your business page needs to be done by a professional. Whether it's a headshot of your face, or a snazzy new logo, it's essential to your Facebook marketing success that it be professional. Use Canva to crop it properly using the correct dimensions so that your head or logo isn't appearing distorted or cut off in the profile picture box. Facebook profile photos have specific size dimensions so it's important that your photo fits. Have you ever gone to someone's page and their profile picture had half of their head cut off? Yeah, that's not professional, and your clients and potential clients will see that and immediately be turned off.

The "About" Section and Your Short Description

The section of your business page where it indicates a 'short description' is incredibly important. This is what populates in searches and on your feed as a default summary of your page. So let's make sure you get this right! You should most definitely include a clear and interesting description of what you do, who you help, and how you help them. Don't forget to include a link to your website in here as well!

The "About" Section and Your Long Description

This section is where you'll highlight the benefits of your services and how you help your clients. Try to include as many relevant keywords in this section as you can, as it'll help you pop up on searches within Facebook itself.

Website Accessibility

The perfect Facebook marketing strategy is based on getting a flow of traffic to a location where leads can be collected and dumped into a sales funnel. That location is most likely a landing page on your website, so we want to make it very easy for visitors of your business page to get to your website/landing page. Include a link to this page in as many places on your Facebook business page as you can.

For instance, it should appear:
- Within the description of your cover photo
- In all of your posts
- In your about sections (short & long)
- In the business information section
- Anywhere else you can squeeze it in!

Cross Promote Your Personal & Business Pages

When you fill out the 'work' section of your personal profile, include a link to your Facebook business page. This way you'll have all of your bases covered and more of your network will be able to find your business page organically.

Routinely Clean Up Your Business Page

Sometimes we post about something and for one reason or another, the post was a dud. No one commented, very few liked it and it just looks bad to have that kind of stuff on your timeline. Do a routine check up for spam comments and posts that didn't get any activity and delete them. Trust me, no one will notice it's gone and your page will be better for it.

Before you dust off your timeline and move on, take note of the types of posts that were duds. Was it the post itself? Or did you just post at the wrong time? Be mindful before you clean it out for good.

2. What The Hell Is A Sales Funnel?

Introduction To How This Works

Using Facebook and social media to connect with and create relationships with your audience is obviously the foundation to any good marketing strategy. If you've got that down and you're ready to scale your marketing efforts and really start generating business from these efforts, it's time to implement a *Sales Funnel*.

Step 1: The Facebook Ad or Top Of Funnel

The top of the funnel is what your visitors will see first, and it's got to be attention grabbing. This can come from one or all of the following suggestions, but it must have a clickable link which leads them to the second step of the sales funnel.

Some good places to originate traffic are:

Facebook Ads
Facebook Posts

Direct Chats/Messages
The clickable tab on your Facebook business page cover

Step 2: Opt-In Offers

How do they work? Why am I giving stuff away for free here? I'm trying to run a business, not a charity.

Relax and let me explain, would ya?!

An opt-in is the baseline offer you're advertising to cold leads to entice them to sign up for your email list. The second step after the initial Facebook ad is the opt-in part of the funnel. This is the proverbial doughnut dangling in front of the running treadmill. Clients reaching out for quick value and easy results.

This will be the reason why your "lead generation page" works and converts. The reason someone will come across your landing page is because they are interested in the opt-in product or service that you have to offer. It entices the client to give you their info in hopes of getting free information and value in exchange.

A great opt-in usually has a strong reference to the service or product which you're hoping they purchase, and teases the results of what buying the higher end product will be.

This step is included within the top of the funnel, and it's where you gather the lead's contact information, in exchange for something they "opt-in" to receive.. Once they've clicked the link in your tab, ad, post, or message they should be lead directly to a landing page or website. This page needs to include a way for you to gather their contact information – this is usually by using some sort of lead form.

You need to give them a reason to give you their contact

information, so in return, you have to solve the problem posed in step one. This page should be clean, concise, and not filled with lots of words or distractions. Make the opt-in form the focus and make sure to let them know what they're getting in return for providing their contact information.

If your landing page isn't converting (people aren't opting-in) you need to refine your offer and incentive. The incentive should be valuable and relevant to your audience.

Here are some ideas for an opt-in offer:
Downloadable Guide
eBook
Free Webinar Training
Consultation, Audit, or Appointment
Local vendor list
Event Invite
Basically any piece of valuable information in any form, that someone wants to receive for free that is in alignment with the services or products you offer.

Once they've opted in, you need a way to deliver the free download immediately. You can use an automated email service like Mailchimp to accomplish the opt-in form and delivery all in one. LeadPages and Clickfunnels are other great programs to use to create your landing page and opt-in forms, and it can also be synched with your email autoresponder to shoot out that welcome email after the visitors signs up for your opt-in offer. Clickfunnels also has their own email autoresponder program within the website, although I don't personally use it with my business. I prefer to use Mailchimp or Constant Contact for my automated email campaigns.

I also like to include a scheduling link at the bottom of all my automated emails, that prompts the person receiving the email to book a call or appointment with me once they see I delivered on the value I promised. By doing this, you are able to weed out the serious people from those who are just looking around for free info. We will go over this more in Step 3.

Another way to set up your ad to acquire someone's contact info, is to create a Lead Generation ad within Facebook itself, instead of a Traffic based ad, which points to a landing page.. It's literally just a different type of ad template that Facebook has created to keep users on their website instead of clicking away. The Lead Generation ad has worked extremely well for myself and my clients, since Facebook will definitely show these ads more often if they keep users on their platform, as opposed to clicking off. It is a simple 2 step ad, that typically has the visitor's correct contact info automatically generated within when they go to sign up for your opt-in offer. Basically whichever email they used to sign up for their Facebook account will be automatically inputted into the correct box. You can even ask for the visitor to submit their phone number within a Lead Generation ad, and the phone number linked to their account will be automatically generated as well. I have tested this on my own ads, and actually got a higher conversion rate when asking for a phone number as opposed to not. Just know that with this type of ad, any questions you ask the user to answer within the lead generation form MUST be answered. Meaning, if you ask for a phone number within the ad, the visitor HAS TO provide it, or they cannot sign up. So this is something you might want to test first vs. just asking to sign up with name and email, and see what performs better for you. It also depends on the type of opt-in offer you're incentivising their contact info with, and what specific business you have, but play around with what will work best for you and your business.

Book, buy, or BYE!
Wasting time trying to appeal to every person and

overwhelm yourself with too many offers and ideas is a surefire way to lose control of your content and funnel entirely.

One step at a time. Especially if you're building this all by yourself. You wouldn't hold an art show before making the paintings. Don't let your funnels spiral out of control.

Start small. Brainstorm what it is you can provide best and easiest at first to get feet in the door, how you can target people who have a problem which your business solves, and take the time to show them how working with you is the best way to get the results they desire and the solution to the problem they are facing.

Whether it's as immediate as going to a restaurant for a great deal, or it's being a personal trainer and signing a client on for a year's worth of training, you're solving a problem in one way or another.

So your opt-in offer should be in extreme alignment with your business model and offers. In short, don't offer advice on things you have to research yourself just because you think it might appeal to a wider audience. If you're not actually an expert in an area, don't pretend you are. Misleading people is another sure-fire way to ensure your marketing fails completely. You are doing this to establish yourself as the expert and the go-to person. People can see right through someone who is faking the funk for a buck. Don't be that person, please.

The options are unlimited, and this is the creative freedom part of running a business that most people strive for. Take the time to really think about what you're looking to offer. In the future, you can always add more or switch things out as your business evolves, but to begin, you're going to want to offer something that is consistently provided in your business. Meaning, what is your most purchased product or service? Create an opt-in and future content that plays to this service.

As previously mentioned, every business should have this sort of intro offer that turns cold leads into customers, and having a product to sell that is "evergreen" and digital goods are a great way to make sales funnels an extremely successful means of income for your business.

The Landing Page

Your landing page is literally where your client will "land" after seeing your ad, or be directed to it from your social media content.

The 2 Basic Types of Landing Pages Are:
THE LEAD GENERATION PAGE
&
THE CLICK THROUGH PAGE

The Lead Generation Page:

This is the type of page you want to use in your funnel to collect information, usually the name and email of your viewer, in exchange for whatever it is you're going to give away to them (Opt-In). This will allow you the opportunity to build your email list and use your email to further market to and nurture your clients, talk to them about your offers, and communicate with them about their wants and needs.

The Click Through Page:

The point of a click through page, is to provide the viewer with valuable content and information before registering for or buying anything. They will start with this page, and "click through" to a following page within your funnel that will direct them to a sales page or checkout page.

A click through page is the best method of introducing your product to the viewer, without automatically asking for an opt-in, or sending them directly to a checkout page from whichever cold ad they came from.

In most people, this kind of approach kind of turns them off, but for those very unique, once in a lifetime type of products, or those funny/ironic items, they tend to work well on incorporated with Facebook ads. People figure they should just buy now because they may never come across the ad again. There's really no way to tell what will work best until you try.

Testing landing pages against each other will give you the best idea of what will work best in your funnel. It really only takes several days to come to a result of what's converting better. When you find your groove, run with it and build it out!

Step 3: Email Automation and Segmentation

Now that you've collected their information and delivered some value, it's time to segment them. Not all of your leads will benefit from the same information. Create segments for your leads and send each segment the information that's most relevant to them. If you're in real estate, your segments might include: buyers, sellers, first time home buyers, renters, etc.

This also is helpful to do when you are able to view which of those who have signed up have actually opened the email, clicked the link within the email, called or emailed to schedule an appointment, etc. You are able to segment those audiences differently into new email lists, and cater what you send them based on their activity. This is how a new funnel pipeline is created! I like to think of a sales funnel as a pipeline, where there is your main means of acquiring their info (the sink) and whatever flows into it, gets channeled through a different pipeline depending on their activity and anticipated outcome. It gets to be fun, and it also dramatically increases productivity within your business, as you are now able to filter out those who are serious about working with you, from those who just want free information online. Regardless, you need to treat every lead with equal attention. They are all possible closed customers one day.

Step 4: Follow Up and Upselling

It typically takes seven touches for a lead to start to trust you. So giving up after step 3 would be a complete waste of your time and money. Step four is all about nurturing that lead, and doing this until the lead becomes an actual client. Once or twice a week, send them useful information and offer to help. Do this until you feel like they're warming up and getting closer to making a decision to work with you. There's no reason why you can't send a personal email to someone who has signed up and engaged with your email, and asking them where they are in their process, and if they had any questions or would be open to getting on a call with you to discuss.

Step 5: Be Consistent and Ask For The Sale

Once you've warmed them up in step four, you've provided them with valuable information, you've answered their questions, and you've gained their trust, it's time to sell! Ask for their business! Ask for the meeting. If you get a no, go back to step four, rinse, and repeat. If you get a maybe, segment them into the "maybe" section, and answer more questions; find out what's holding them back from making a decision.

Once you get a sizable segmented list of people that have

gone through your sales funnel, take a step back and analyze your performance.

Ask yourself...

Which (Step 1) content attracted the most attention?

Which (Step 2) landing page layouts and verbiage converted best?

Which (Step 2) opt-in offers converted best?

Which (Step 4) value based messages/emails created the most engagement?

Which questions you received in (Step 4) were asked the most? Use those for your next (Step 1) posts, ads, tabs and your next (Step 2) free opt-in offers.

Which objections did you receive the most in (Step 5)? Answer those early on in your next sales funnel.

3. THE WHAT & WHY

Introduction

Remember why you're doing this…

Always keep your "why" and your story close to you when creating your content. Keep your business goals in mind throughout the whole process. Falling off the program is totally normal for most people, but make sure you come pick back up. The quicker you start getting your funnel running, the quicker your income goals and dreams can become a reality.

After all, your clients are going to be buying into YOU. Never be ashamed of where you've come from. Use your story as business fuel. Focus on where you want to go and let that be your motivation. Running a business can be hard, but don't get discouraged! It doesn't have to be, and I'm here to help you get things running as smoothly as possible, as quickly as possible, from the beginning.

Every great success story once endured a struggle…

Champions don't make comebacks, they overcome

setbacks.

The What

You should start thinking about WHAT it is you're looking to sell and WHAT service you're looking to provide.

At the absolute beginning side of your sales funnel, you'll be needing an offer to present to those who come across your ads. An offer that is too good to pass up, and somewhat of an impulse sign up or buy, based on their targeting categories.

IT COULD BE ANYTHING.

Obviously, I can never guarantee that what works for one person will work for someone else. Just be consistent, work hard, be diligent, and the work you do will pay off. I promise you.

The Why

Why did you buy this book?

Are you starting a new business and need help building out your brand and attaining new leads?

Looking to sell a product or service and have to start advertising but you don't know how to start and don't want to go to an agency?

Been burned by a marketing company before and just don't want to go through that again?

Are you looking to grow your own digital marketing agency and learn how to build out sales funnels for clients?

Or maybe you just want to learn the basics of digital marketing for your existing business?

Whatever the reason is, going through this book and absorbing and implementing the materials I'll teach you, you'll learn what it will take to get to your advertising up and running and hit your income goals.

My "why" came after leaving college early, attempting and quitting several business endeavors, starting and restarting multiple times as a real estate agent, and realizing I was setting myself up for disaster with every entrepreneurial attempt I was making. I never gave myself the time to learn the very important marketing systems that would eventually shift my business, so inevitably I was doomed from the start. I didn't have the systems in place, nor did I know that they even existed at the time, so there really was no easy way for these ideas I had to actually work without a great system set up. I needed to start thinking like an actual business owner and boss, not just a want-repreneur.

I was naive about what it would take to be successful, and after seeing so many other people I looked up to consistently killing it every time they tried something, I only became more and more frustrated. Frustrated, but determined to figure it all out.

Implementing a system like the one you're about to learn has literally turned my leads on autopilot and given me the freedom and flexibility to work where I want, when I want, and not have to worry about getting sick, taking a vacation or just needing time off, because I know my business is running on its own.

I fired my boss and now I am one.

You're about to create a well oiled lead generating machine.

You're about to turn your lead faucet on.

Are you ready?
Let's Do This.

4. FACEBOOK ADS CREATION

Ahhh, our beloved Facebook ads.

Well, they're beloved to me, at least!

And now, I'm going to make you love them too!

Yes, I'm going to MAKE YOU love Facebook ads.

To start off, having awesome Facebook Ads is both a skill and an art form. You must be in tune with your customer and what they're looking for when creating an ad. Being communicative and making sure you're on the same page is first and foremost.

Being specific about your typical customer is important as well, as the people and interests you target are going to be the reason your ads work or not. It's also important to note that there are certain guidelines you must abide by in order to legally create Facebook ads. Some categories are not allowed, even to the point of certain "risque" photos being blocked or having ad accounts shut down. (Facebook is very finicky about ad approvals at times.)

THIS IS NOTHING TO FEAR.

Getting an ad account shut down doesn't happen unless you continually make the same mistakes and try to get away with it. Facebook is the Eye in the Sky that knows all, so please play kind if you want your business to be successful.

The Setup

To begin, you're going to obviously need a:
1) Facebook account & Facebook Business Account
2) Facebook business page

Head over to Business.Facebook.com and login. The steps go sequentially so there's no reason to worry.

All you'll be doing at this point is integrating your Facebook Page with the Facebook business account you're going to use to run ads. The Facebook Business Manager is the website that mostly everything involving your ads and page management will be done under.

Please, please, PLEASE do not login to Facebook traditionally and try to navigate to the business page that way. Facebook has been flagging accounts that they see are being run as business pages under personal accounts, and making you have to login through the Business.Facebook.com site from now on to create and edit ads and some content.

Don't risk having your page or ad campaigns deleted because you tried to login the backwards way. Do it right from the beginning. We're not in the business of cutting corners. It doesn't save time at all. In fact, you'll most likely regret not having done it the right way from the beginning. Get yourself in the habit of doing it this way.

I'm going to assume you already have both of those set up at this point, so let's move into setting up your Ads account.

After you sign in to Business.Facebook.com, click on the business you want to access, which will open up your Business Manager. From here, you can click the menu on top to access your billing. You want to set this up before creating your first ad. On this page, if your ads account is setup already, you can simply click your ad account and be taken to the Ads Manager page, which is where you will create and access all of your campaigns.

Now, while you're in your ads account, you're going to want to set up your account role permissions. Account Role Permissions are the people on your team who you are also giving access to your ads account to. Keep in mind, many people hire out a Facebook Ads expert to save time and money creating strong ads, but for the sake of creating a complete sales funnel, I will be going through the basic and important steps to making a kick ass ad.

Keep in mind that Facebook charges either once a budget is reached, or sporadically during the lifetime of your campaign if you're running a campaign with no end date. In the beginning, there will be an automatic threshold for billing until you make your first several payments. After you prove that you're a legitimate account and have no billing hiccups, Facebook allows you to increase the threshold to an amount of your liking and be billed once you reach that set amount, as opposed to every few days, whenever Facebook wants to bill you.

Ok, so your billing is set up!

Now you can head over to your account settings, under the top left Menu tab again.

Click "All Tools" and click the "Settings" link.

Now, you can add account roles to whoever you want on your team that you want to give account access to.

If it's just you running the ads, you can skip this step.

This is the basic setup of your ads account. The next chapter will show you how we are going to build out our first ad!

Creating Your First Ad

Okay, so we got your account all set up, and it's ready to start producing, but are you?

BREATHE IN & OUT.
BREATHE IN AGAIN.
Let's begin.

OK, so maybe you've tried running an ad campaign in the past and maybe you were less than happy with the success you received. To me, it's like going to cosmetology school for a haircut. It might turn out great, but wouldn't you rather work with a professional?

I thought so. Let's get to learning, ok?

Facebook Ads are constantly being updated with new and exciting features, but the main build-out of each feature is relatively the same.

So to begin, we are going to start with your simple Video or Photo ad that sends users to a website link. This is called a Traffic ad.

These are the best types of ads to start off with, because they are the most fuss-free of all the different options Facebook is giving us, and the easiest to learn with. Truthfully, you should have one of these ads running at all times, as long as it's converting well.

Start by clicking the "Create Ad" button you'll see on your Ads Account homepage.

From here, you're going to be prompted to pick your campaign objective, and will see many different options.

Since we're building a sales funnel, we need to direct ad traffic to our landing page. Click the "Traffic" button, and enter in the name of the campaign you're going to use. This is for your eyes only, so you can tell the difference between ads in your Ads Manager.

Now, you're going to be asked about TARGETING.

Targeting and Placements

This is when things get kind of awesome.

You've chosen and named your campaign.

Now you're being asked to target people.

Facebook has some of the best targeting features available on all social media platforms.

It's actually astounding how on point it is.

So since this is the first audience you're going to be making, you will not have any "saved audiences" to worry about, so you're going to want to create a "custom audience."

When creating your audience, you're going to want to figure out:

The location you're looking to target
Where these people are likely hanging out online?
What are their interests?
Who are your main competitors?
All the demographics of your ideal client.

The reason we get so detailed in the sense of looking into demographics, is because there really is no point in showing your ad to EVERYONE on Facebook, because EVERYONE is not your ideal customer!

If you have the ability to save money, have a lower CPC (Cost Per Click) and get in front of people who actually like and want your products and services, wouldn't that be smarter than wasting money on pointless clicks that lead nowhere?

This is why Facebook Ads are so magical.

With proper targeting, you are doing your business such a favor because as long as your content is in line, these people are going to love what you provide!

While entering in the details of who you want to target, the "Suggested" feature will be your best friend. It will give you great options for similar interests, demographics & ways of reaching people.

Keep in mind that real estate ads cannot go against Fair Housing policies, so you have to get a little more creative with your targeting. I find that advertising a guide or a phone call opportunity works much better than advertising a listing.

You can enter many different options, but make sure the lever on the right side of the page moves from BROAD closer to SPECIFIC. Anywhere in the middle of the green is usually optimal in the beginning. The more broad your ad is, the lower your relevance score will usually be, and the less Facebook will show your ads.

Facebook also lets you decide if you want to run an indefinite campaign or a campaign under a certain time frame. Along with those options, you can also create a split test for your ads to test different audiences, photos and ad copy.

But back to building your basic ad...
You've got your targeting done, saved the audience to possibly use in the future, and now you're being asked where you want to place your ads.

Placements

To start off, I always suggest using the Automatic Placements feature, so Facebook can use its magic to decide where it feels your ads will perform best. If you are looking to run an exclusive Facebook based desktop campaign, you'd select that option here at this time. But for the sake of moving along and getting comfortable building an ad, choose the Automatic Placements feature.

In the future, as you get more and more comfortable with creating ads, you'll want to test the different placements and see where your ads and the different type of creative content you make performs best, and gives you the best run for your money.

Another thing to keep in mind, is that if you're creating a video to show within your ad, the length of the video will determine its placements. Be smart with what you create if you want your ad to be shown and placed in different areas. We know that Facebook and Instagram work together, and there are many placements available among the 2 social media platforms, so choosing the place you think you will find the most success, or the place you have the larger following might be the best move.

Side Note: If you have over 10K followers on your Instagram page, you can also use the "swipe up" feature within your stories, and this is a great place to speak about your opt-in offer and give people easy access to sign up for it, without having to spend any money on that ad at all.

Your best bet is to make your video 60 seconds or less, and run that on Facebook and Instagram, and creating a shorter 15 second version that you test as a separate campaign, which can be shown on the stories exclusively. But find what works best for you! I'm just here to provide you with some ideas.

Writing Copy and Creative

Moving right along…

Up next is choosing your ad's creative, and actually MAKING the ad! Congrats!

You've made it to the most important part of building your Facebook ad without hopefully having a panic attack or getting overwhelmed…

I told you I was going to make you LOVE Facebook Ads! They're easier than you give them credit for!

Okay, so now this is the fun part, or at least it is to me.

We are going to start by picking your ad format type.

I suggest using a Single Image or a Single Video to begin.
Carousel ads work best when advertising several related products, like if you have a t-shirt store. Just keep in mind, anyone can run a Facebook ad. It's the process of integrating it into your sales funnel that makes it that much more powerful.

You should have your ad's graphics made ahead of time so it's ready to go with your ad when this time comes.

Facebook also HATES when ad photos have too much text on them. Some is okay (about 20% of the photo can contain text and Facebook will probably still show your ad.) Anything more than that, and Facebook probably won't even approve your ad, so only write what's absolutely necessary on your photos, and leave the rest for the ad copy itself.

Facebook can be a bit temperamental, so please, if your ad gets rejected at first, try, try again. It could be as something as small as saying the word "DETOX" when talking about a skinny detox tea, not a drug detox. But the word itself might trigger Facebook's filters and need a manual review, so just be prepared for that.

I once ran an ad campaign for a meal replacement drink, and Facebook gave me the hardest time approving my ads because the website the ad directed to said things like "skinny", "fat", and had photos of women in bikinis. It can be a challenge, but if you plan for this you can work around it easily.

The photo or video you choose should literally make people stop mid-scroll to see what it is you have to offer. This is called a "Pattern Disrupt." Just how I got you to click my ad and get you to buy this book, your ad should be able to do the same thing.

Again, if you hate making graphics, Canva is a great option with its vast selection of pre made templates and is perfect when you're in a pinch, don't have a graphic designer, and need to get something made quickly.

Use the right image size (1200 x 628 pixels), so that your ad creatives look good on every screen

After you've decided on the format and content you want to use, you're going to move onto writing your actual ad.

Copywriting

Your ad copy can either make or break your ad, and should resonate very strongly with how your target audience feels, how they would speak, and kind of pushes the knife into their pain-points just enough to keep them intrigued and wanting to sign up for your opt-in, while still providing some value and leaving room for them to want more.

If writing isn't your thing, find someone who is good at creating compelling copy. Spelling and grammatical errors will make you lose legitimacy, very quickly. Proofread and double check what you write for errors.

Also, it's important that your ad is not too long or too short. Emojis also work great within an ad to bring some attention to those scrolling, but keep in mind, that depending on the placement of the ads, the emojis may or may not show up. This is why it's sometimes smarter to create different ads per platform.

Different Platform
Different Audience
Different Message & Marketing Approach

As previously stated, Facebook Ads are both a skill and an art form, so be open to testing different things until you find something that sticks and converts well for you.

There's nothing wrong with running the same ad copy several times while testing different photos and audience targeting.

Find what works for you and your business.

After your ad is built out, hit the SUBMIT button on the bottom of the screen, and allow your ad to go through the Facebook review process. This can take anywhere from 15 minutes to a few hours to approve, but once your ads are live, they can start converting immediately.

Something good to keep in mind before getting totally disheartened after 1 day of running ads without anything converting, is that Facebook will take about a week or so to go through what's called the "learning phase" of running the ads. This is when they will show ads to whoever you have in your targeting, but really figure out who is engaging with your ads and show it to more people who are similar to that audience.

After you write your copy, you are going to have to also be sure that you include the link to your landing page within the website section. The Facebook Ad should be the last thing you create in your sales funnel. Start from the finish line and reverse engineer your way back to your ad. This way, you aren't running around like a chicken without a head trying to get everything set up in a pinch so your Facebook ads can go live.

5. THE DO'S & DON'TS OF SOCIAL MEDIA

Posting Frequency & Engagement

If you only follow one rule, let it be this one. Keep 80% of your Facebook content value based. That means it should be social, helpful, or interesting to your audience; content worth engaging with. The other 20% of your Facebook content can include self promotion, selling, and whatever else you see fit.

Post frequency should be kept to 1-2 posts per day. Some people believe in posting as little as 1-4 times per week. I see that as a bit low considering the social environment we live in these days. You want to teeter the fine line of providing value consistently, and spamming and overwhelming people with too much info. Any more than 2 posts per day leads to unfollows. Over 80% of people say they love to find and follow brands on Facebook but of those, almost 50% say they hate when brands clutter their newsfeed, so be wise and selective with what you post. If you're unsure if it would make a good post, don't do it. Only post about what will be valuable to your audience and your brand itself.

Don't ignore your audience once you've worked so hard to create valuable and engaging content. The point of Facebook marketing is to generate conversations that lead to more business. So once you've published a post, be vigilant and responsive to any interaction at all. This means responding to comments, answering questions, "liking" people's comments, and also engaging on THEIR posts, so you show that you're more than just a social media posting machine, but there's also a human behind the computer (or phone) screen, and you can relate to their world as well.

Type of Content to Post on Your Facebook Page

It's important to keep your Facebook business page filled with fresh content that your followers will either find helpful, interesting, or both. Finding relevant and fun content isn't really that difficult if you make a plan.

If you're a local service based business, fine tuning your Facebook marketing to include a local focus can be a game changer for you. Most of your business will come from and live in your local market and they can be easily reached with strategic Facebook marketing strategies.

Let's go over a few awesome (and easy) ways you can tap into this.

Use local videos and images within your posts. The goal here is to connect with your local audience by documenting and promoting local things, events and places that you have in common. Find a few photographers that would be open and excited to have their work shared on your page, and in exchange you'll tag them in the post. They'll get more exposure and you'll get into their followers' news feed, especially if they share the post to their personal and business pages. Everybody wins!

Always cross promote and tag others in your posts when

possible. If you're posting about a new business opening, tag their business page and the owner's personal page. This is three fold. You'll drastically improve visibility of your content (and your business), the owners will likely share this post to their network, further increasing your reach, and you'll make your post much more helpful to your audience by giving them an accessible way to reach this exciting new business.

Feature your customers and fans. If you've got a client (past or present) that's done something really special, won an award, completed a marathon, got married, or had any other special achievement or life event, give them a shoutout and tag them. This type of post is a great way to spread the love, connect deeper with your clients, and it'll get way more engagement than your other posts. Their family and friends will comment, share, and get to know you and this, my friend, is Facebook marketing gold!

Post a general thank you to your clients or vendors you've worked with in the past year. You can thank the group as a whole, no tags necessary. Always include a photo – making it a personal family photo is even better. This should come from your heart. If you can make this a video, even better.

Join local Facebook groups. Facebook groups are one place that lots of people are hanging out in. (More on this below.) It's a safe space for people who share a specific interest to gather & share information, ask questions, and grow relationships. It's the perfect place for you to gather information on what your ideal client's biggest problems are as well. Get in there, listen, and provide helpful information that will help them solve their problems. DO NOT sell in a Facebook group. You will get kicked out immediately. Just be helpful and be yourself.

Local awareness posts are a good way to become a source

of information and gain trust and credibility within your local market. Types of local awareness posts may include public safety announcements, upcoming road construction projects, information on neighborhood watch associations, and things along those lines.

Enable reviews on your Facebook business page. We live in a review culture and this is a quick way for you to collect positive feedback. (I am extremely ANTI Yelp Ads, because of their scummy tactics when you don't buy marketing.)

A good way to increase reviews on your page is to offer past clients a $5 Starbucks gift card or something small in exchange for a review. It's also important to note that reviews don't always have to be about your business, itself. Having friends and family write a character review about you as a person works as well. This way, you are able to have people who haven't yet worked with you, but who know, like, and trust you, write a review for you.

Collaborate with local businesses when you run out of ideas. There are endless ways to do this. Starting with the businesses that your audience frequents or has interest in is a good place to start. I love to do a blog post on how the small Mom & Pop companies in my city started and then share it all over my social media platforms. This gets right to the core of your city and your community and it's a great way to connect with real people in your local market. More Facebook Gold!

Optimize Your Facebook Page for Search Engines

AKA: SEO. People use Facebook as a search engine just as much as Google or Pinterest. To make your Business page easier to find, you've got to focus on improving your SEO (Search Engine Optimization).

Start by using relevant keywords that your audience would be searching for in your posts, your business page description, and your about me sections. This will help you stand out in the vast sea of Facebook Business pages in your industry.

Complete 100% of your business page info. Facebook algorithms will reward you for including all necessary business information. It's a way to be found easier, and build credibility all at once.

How to Raise Your Engagement Rates

The name of the Facebook Marketing game is to generate business which means your content strategy has to be based on engagement. Engagement increases exposure, sparks conversation, builds relationships, grows your following, and gets you more business. So let's talk about exactly how you can raise your engagement rates!

Add photos to all of your posts. By including a professional and eye catching (but not cheesy) photo to your post, you can expect 53% more likes, 84% more click-throughs, and 104% more comments. Boom.

Keep your posts informative. There's a fine line between providing too much information and too little. You don't want the copy in your caption to be a novel, but you also don't want it to look like you couldn't be bothered to write. If you can't take the time to write a good caption for your posts, hire someone who can. In the age of social media, people see captions and decide right then and there if you can be trusted with their business. If you aren't a good writer, there are plenty of people who can do this for you for a small amount of money. The best thing to do if you're stuck with caption writing, and find that this is a problem that you come across quite often, is to hire someone to create your social media posts for the next month. This way, you don't have to worry about what to post everyday, and can better utilize that time elsewhere in your business.

Simply find someone whose work you like, and find out how to work with them. You can relay over the important information, photos, and events you want to include within that month's content, and leave the rest to the writer to create.

Post questions, preferably quirky questions or ones with limited answers. This will usually yield you much more comments than if you were to post a fact or other tid-bit of information.

If there's a special coupon or discount on a local service that you have access to, share that with your audience. You can expect lots of shares and more page likes.

Run a contest and make the entry a page like/comment/share. About 35% will be your 'like rate'; but you can increase this by using highly effective words in your contest post like: winner, win, contest, entry, enter, and promotion.

Use emojis and emoticons in your Facebook marketing posts. Have fun with this, but try to make them at least a little relevant/appropriate for your audience. Facebook posts that include emoticons receive roughly 57% more likes, 33% more shares, and 33% more comments. Pretty crazy how these insights exist.

When you want to have conversations with your Facebook audience, try to use the Chat feature instead of emails. The response rate is much, much higher because of the nature of the App itself. It's more informal, less sales-y, and you can see when they've received and read the message

– something most emails platforms don't provide, and are incredibly inaccurate when they actually do.

Facebook Groups

A Facebook group is not a profile or a business page. It's also not an event page. What it is, is a place for a specific list of people to share photos, links, discussions, updates, and more.

There are three types of groups:

Public – Anyone can search and join
Closed – Anyone can search but need permission from a group member to join
Secret – No one outside of the group can search or join without an invite from within the group

As with general social media posting, many of the same rules apply, but Facebook Groups have quickly become a great place to share your message, provide value, build legitimacy, and shop for clients all at the same time.

There are tons of Facebook Groups online, but the key is being strategic about where you're posting, when, and how. For example, if you're a business coach, it will be easy to find a group for business coaches, yet, it might not be the best place to find a new client.

Unless, of course, the business coaches in that group need a business coach themselves. Not impossible of course, but the results may be less than what you'd hoped for.

Whereas, if you're a business coach, finding a group for small business owners, where you can meet people in all different industries, and be able to provide value occasionally and answer questions will definitely be a better group to build your credibility and find new clients in. In fact, when being consistent in certain groups and showing up to help others, I've had dozens of people actually message me and ask how they can find more info about working together.

Don't ever message people asking for them to check out your product or service without previously speaking to them and knowing that they're in the market for something you can help them with. There is nothing more tacky or annoying than a person asking you to check out their website or offer after never having spoken to them before that. I usually just ignore their messages and sometimes even block them if they're over the top. Definitely not a good way to make a first impression. Network Marketers, take note. Nothing makes my eyes roll back more than a girl from high school who I haven't spoken to in 15 years sending me a "Hey Girl" message followed by a sales pitch for essential oils or waist wraps. Hard pass.

If it works for you, starting your own group might be a good idea to share your products and services while helping others and establishing yourself as an authority figure. If you have enough people online who are interested, I say go for it! It's free advertising for you and you never know, there could be a huge market for your type of group. This way, you make your own rules and can do as you please.

Facebook groups are a great way for you to prospect and do lots of business if you can handle it correctly. Basically you'll want to think of a category or type of group you'd like to create yourself. This could be a specific neighborhood, local mom's group, bar owners group, or any group of people that have one thing in common. Take the time to research what's out there, and mimic what's working for others.

The main goal of the group is to encourage interaction

between members and provide lots and lots of value to them on a consistent basis. Simply put, be helpful, be active, and use the 80/20 rule. Eighty percent of the time you'll want to be helping; the other twenty percent can be selling or asking for business.

Another way to scale your success from Facebook groups is to find convos in the feed, research the problem, write a blog post about the solution, and share that blog post in the group feed.

You'll always want to be adding quality members to the group so share it with anyone you see fit and encourage members to do the same on a regular basis.

The one thing to keep in mind with Facebook groups, is if it's not your personal group that you created yourself, make sure you follow the group's rules for posting. Many groups are no-sell groups, meaning you are not allowed to advertise in the group, but that doesn't mean you can't find clients. Providing information, value, and help to those within the group will establish you as a thought leader and expert, and this in turn helps with referrals and with people organically seeking you out for your expertise and experience. Don't be fearful of doing a little bit of work if it means getting clients and closed deals at the end of the day. Play the long game on social media. Nothing worth having comes easily, or quickly for that matter.

A smart way to do it is after someone signs up for your opt-in, within that initial email that is automatically sent to them, provide them with a link to your Facebook Group. Explain to them how it's a great place to be in contact with you, and where you will be sharing lots of inside tips and hacks to help them. You can create a group for mostly anything! So find a group idea that works well for your business and get to it!

Please don't automatically add people though. Make them come to you. I can't tell you the amount of times I've been manually added to a Facebook group without even knowing who the person who added me was. I had no reason to be in this group at all, and it was all a numbers game to this person. A great way to get deleted, in my opinion.

Many groups have strict rules and guidelines and have a strict no messing up policy, as well. They have specific days for posting about your business, like "Small Business Saturdays," but a group should usually just be utilized for conversation and community. If you find a group that allows promotional posting, please keep in mind that everyone else is going to be promoting themselves at this time as well. So the odds of what you post being seen at all is slim to none. Your best bet is actually engaging with people and actually caring about them! I know, it's unheard of to care about someone in business…

Not anymore. The days of being self-serving are over. It isn't about you anymore. It's about who you can help. People want to work with PEOPLE at the end of the day. And good business is really just knowing how to interact with people and treat them how you would want to be treated.

6. GRADUATION

YOU DID IT!

Give yourself a huge pat on the back!

You made it through Leads For Days!

And, I hope you're way more clear on how a fully automated sales funnel can and will undoubtedly change your business.

Getting to this point is important. It means you actually committed and dedicated your time and effort to learning something to help improve your business, so don't be surprised that after this first step, the floodgates just open up and some pretty magical things happen in your business.

Sometimes, all it takes is the first step, and the Universe comes and helps you out on your path. You put the energy into growth and it will inevitably be returned back to you.

I am so proud of you for completing this book, and hopefully, for having integrated what you've learned into your business. It's time to see all the rewards of your hard work show up in your bank account.

Where there is a will, there is a way. Get these pages set up and start rolling in the business. It's your time!

I would love to hear your feedback!

What did you find informative? Tell me how this is all working out for you and your business! I'd love to hear about the results you're getting from implementing this system within your business.

If you've only been treating your business like a job, this system will surely help up-level your mindset to that of a business owner now.

A Facebook marketing campaign is the best way to build out your brand at this point in time, as you are able to establish yourself as an expert in your area and industry, and consistently provide people with value and answers for their issues and questions. Regardless of what industry you are in, there are lots of questions and concerns that come up for many of our clients. Being able to be the voice of reason and information for those uneasy clients will make all the difference to them, and to your business.

Do this right, and watch the referrals roll in. Hopefully this all helps you build your business to levels you didn't know were possible. In time, you will be able to take your business from a one-person-show, to a growing team. Leads will be rolling in consistently, and you will no longer have to worry about or stress the need to contact these leads immediately, since the email auto responder system will do that for you!

If there is anything you have a question about, or if you

would like to talk to me personally about running your ad campaigns for your business, please don't hesitate to reach out to me! I always love hearing from people who are on their hustle and hungry to make it work. I know what it's like, and I wish you all the success in the world

ABOUT THE AUTHOR

Christina Friscia is a social media and lead generation expert, currently living in New York. Being able to help businesses achieve new levels of success is one of the greatest joys and pleasures in her life. She created Leads For Days as a way to help service based businesses finally figure out this whole social media game, and set themselves up for success once and for all. A true Capricorn at heart, life is about the climb and getting to the summit is just a part of the story. She created and dedicates this book to every struggling entrepreneur who needs just a little encouragement and push in the right direction. Stay grounded but keep climbing and accept nothing less than success.